YVONNE ROGENMOSER was born in 1977. She is a scientific illustrator and specializes in the communication of knowledge through pictures. As a designer she is interested in anything and everything that can be painted, drawn or illustrated, and her work ranges from cookbooks to maps.
Yvonne Rogenmoser lives and works in Zürich and Versam, Switzerland.

Copyright © 2016 by NordSüd Verlag AG, CH-8005 Zürich, Switzerland.
First published in Switzerland under the title **Über den Gotthard.**
English translation copyright © 2016 by NorthSouth Books, Inc., New York 10016.
English translation by David Henry Wilson.
First published in the United States and Canada in 2016 by NorthSouth Books, Inc., an imprint of Nord-Süd Verlag AG, CH-8005 Zürich, Switzerland.
Distributed in the United States by NorthSouth Books, Inc., New York 10016.
Library of Congress Cataloging-in-Publication Data is available.
ISBN: 978-0-7358-4257-1
Printed in Latvia by Livonia Print, Riga, February 2016
1 3 5 7 9 · 10 8 6 4 2
www.northsouth.com

4358

Crossing the GOTTHARD

YVONNE ROGENMOSER

The Longest Tunnel in the World

North
South

Heading South — "We've been stuck in this traffic jam for 2 hours!"
groaned Dad.
"We're bored!" moaned Emil and Paula.
"I'll be happy if we can just get moving," sighed Dad. "Then we'd be there."
"Oh, stop moaning, all of you," said Mom. "Years ago this journey was a lot harder!"

The Gotthard — The Alps stretch across

Europe like a mighty wall. Since time immortal these mountains have made travel from north to south and vice versa extremely difficult, dangerous, and sometimes even impossible. People soon realized one thing: in order to get across, it was best to find a place that wasn't too high. One such place is the Gotthard in Switzerland.

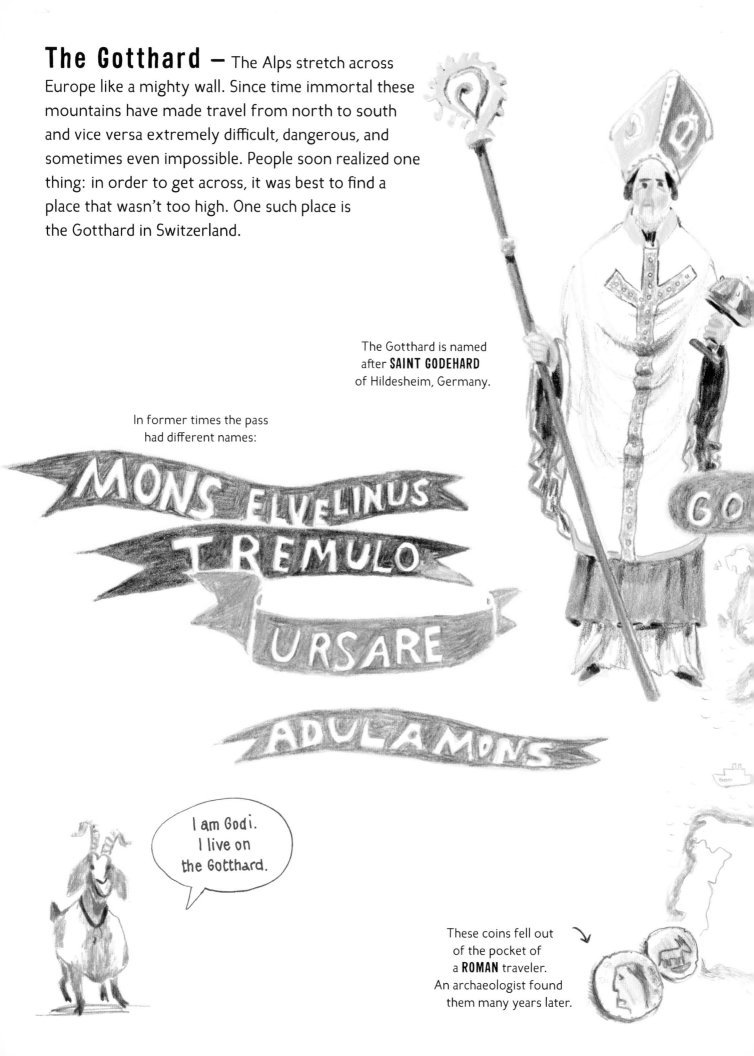

The Gotthard is named after **SAINT GODEHARD** of Hildesheim, Germany.

In former times the pass had different names:

MONS ELVELINUS

TREMULO

URSARE

ADULA MONS

I am Godi. I live on the Gotthard.

These coins fell out of the pocket of a **ROMAN** traveler. An archaeologist found them many years later.

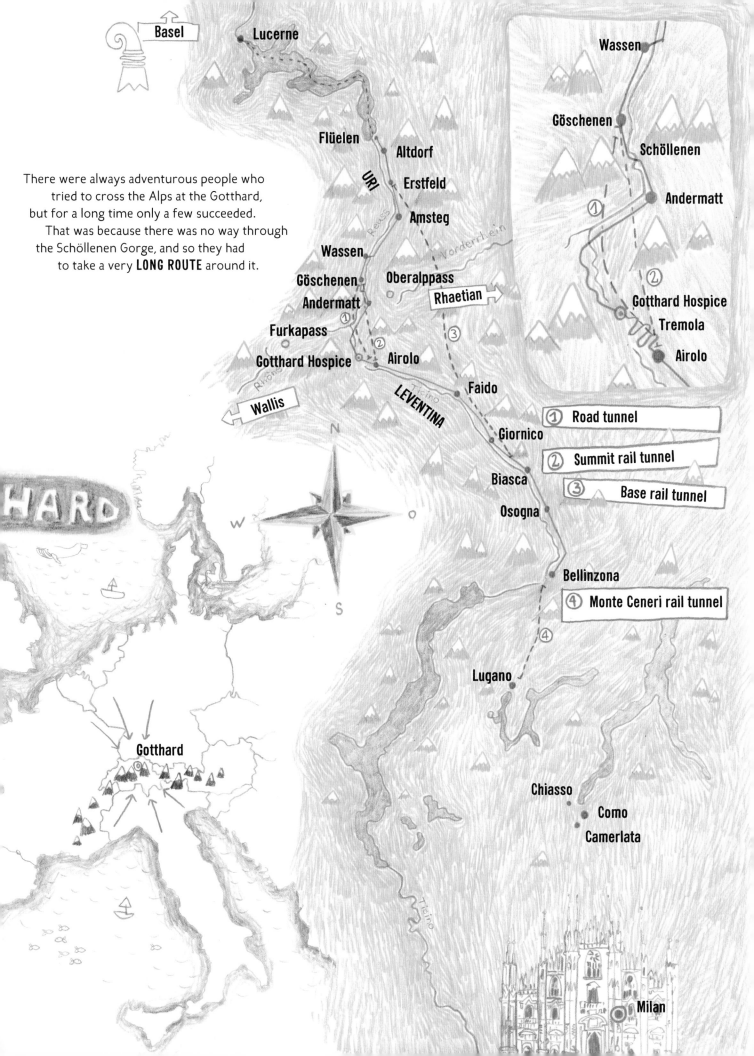

There were always adventurous people who tried to cross the Alps at the Gotthard, but for a long time only a few succeeded. That was because there was no way through the Schöllenen Gorge, and so they had to take a very **LONG ROUTE** around it.

Basel

Lucerne

Flüelen

Altdorf

Erstfeld

Amsteg

URI

Wassen

Göschenen

Andermatt

①

Furkapass

Gotthard Hospice

②

Airolo

Wallis

Oberalppass

Rhaetian

Reuss

Vorderrhein

③

LEVENTINA

Ticino

Faido

Giornico

Biasca

Osogna

Bellinzona

④

Lugano

Chiasso

Como

Camerlata

Milan

HARD

Gotthard

N

W   O

S

Wassen

Göschenen

Schöllenen

Andermatt

①

②

Gotthard Hospice

Tremola

Airolo

① Road tunnel

② Summit rail tunnel

③ Base rail tunnel

④ Monte Ceneri rail tunnel

The Schöllenen Gorge — The route through the Gotthard

would have been ideal: access is easy and the pass is relatively low. However, there is one big obstacle: The Schöllenen Gorge.

The first **PATHS** through the gorge were constructed around 1200, but people were afraid to use them. The turbulence of the River Reuss, the steep rock faces, and the violent spray reminded them of hell. Many a traveler closed his eyes to avoid looking down into the terrifying depths. It was even said that the Devil himself had a hand in building one of the bridges.

THE LEGEND OF THE DEVIL

The people of Uri wanted a path across the Gotthard so that they could get the sweet wine that was made in the south. The canton's councilors therefore held a meeting in the Schöllenen to discuss how they might best overcome the obstacle of the wild gorge. When they stood beside the raging Reuss, it seemed impossible to build a bridge over it.

"Then let the Devil build a bridge!" cried the mayor. No sooner had he uttered these words than the Devil appeared before them, offering them a deal: he would build a bridge, but his fee would be the soul of whoever was first to cross it. "It's not going to be me," thought each of the councilors, and so they all agreed to the arrangement. A few days later, they returned to the gorge, and lo and behold, the bridge had been built. But on the other side sat the Devil, patiently awaiting his reward. Several days passed, and the Devil still sat there waiting, and the people of Uri began to feel uncomfortable. Then a goatherd had a clever idea: "I'll drive my billy goat over the bridge!" And that was exactly what he did.

The Devil was furious. He picked up a huge rock in order to smash the bridge. But just then a little old lady came along the path and painted a cross on the rock. When the Devil saw the cross, he threw the great boulder at the bridge with all his might and departed. But the rock missed the bridge and landed near Göschenen, where it can still be seen today. In all the excitement, nobody paid any attention to the goat, and so he wandered all by himself across the Gotthard. To this day his descendants speak of him with pride and tell his story to the next generation of goats.

Transport

Transport — Thanks to the bridges, the Schöllenen Gorge had at last been conquered and the route across the Gotthard was open. From now on the valleys of Urseren and Leventina became a hive of activity: it was the age of animal-powered transport.

More and more goods were transported across the Gotthard. The local people formed **TRANSPORT AND DISTRIBUTION COOPERATIVES**, and these ensured that the work was allocated fairly and the goods were taken quickly and efficiently across the mountain.

IT IS FORBIDDEN FOR ANYONE TO SLEEP IN THEIR SHOES.

The **SUST** was a warehouse. This was where the goods from the nearest transportation center were delivered and kept safe from the weather and thieves.

The **RUNNERS** [here we see runners from Schwyz] were the early equivalent of our postmen. They were the bearers of all the official news.

The **DISTRIBUTORS** allocated loads to the **DRIVERS**.

MERCHANTS traveled regularly to Milan to conduct their business.

There were also customs posts, where people had to pay a **TOLL** in order to use the tracks. Today one has to buy a motorway permit.

What an inconvenience!

Travelers could spend the night in simple **INNS** or **HOSPICES**.

Poor people were allowed to stay there for free.

A taxi along the mule track: if you could afford it, you could have yourself carried in a sedan chair across the mountain.

This monk had a long journey ahead of him, as he was on a **PILGRIMAGE** to Rome.

The old measure of **1 LOAD** amounted to 330–440 pounds, and it was tied to a pack animal.

Winter —

Winters on the Gotthard are very long. In the old days, the pass was open all year round. Men, women, and children shoveled and wore down a path that could be navigated by sleds.

salt   wine   spices   raw silk

cheese

fabrics of linen and wool

leather and skins

resin

All kinds of goods were transported across the Gotthard. **CATTLE** were the prime export of the people living in the Alpine Valley. They drove the animals across the mountain every autumn. At that time the tracks were barred to the columns of pack animals.

edicinal plants

hardwoods

liquor

minerals

pitch

goats

sheep

pigs

rice

maize

paper

oils

soap

coffee

tobacco

The Stagecoach

The Stagecoach — Not until 1830 was the whole Gotthard pass accessible to vehicles. The stagecoach carried mail and passengers over it. The large coach was generally accompanied by smaller vehicles, and the arrival of the convoy became a real spectacle in every village. The villagers would be informed of the latest news, and they could also gaze in admiration at the ornate hats of the ladies from the city.

It often happened that the passengers quarreled over who should have the **BEST SEATS** in the coach.

The **CONDUCTOR** was responsible for the passengers and the collection and delivery of the mail throughout the journey.

The **COACHMAN** or **POSTILLION** was changed twelve times along the stretch between Flüelen and Camerlata, as were the horses to prevent exhaustion.

TREMOLA ROAD: 37 bends between the hospice and Airolo

Once proper roads had been built across other Swiss passes, such as Simplon and San Bernardino, the Gotthard had to catch up in a hurry if it was to remain competitive.

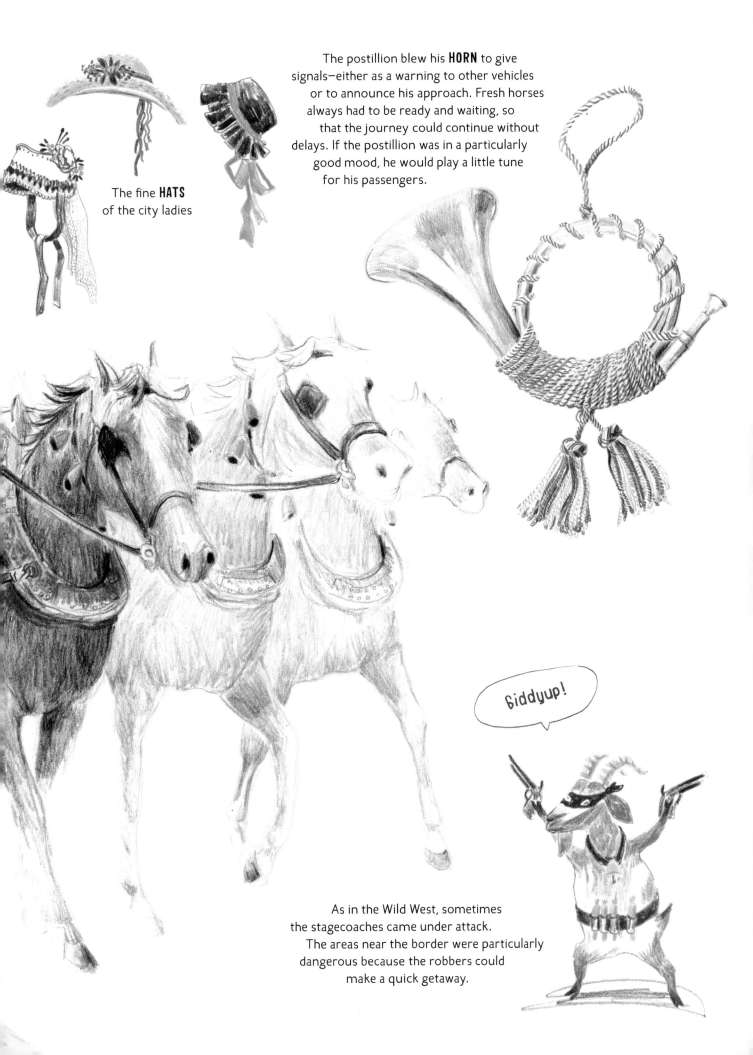

The fine **HATS**
of the city ladies

The postillion blew his **HORN** to give
signals—either as a warning to other vehicles
or to announce his approach. Fresh horses
always had to be ready and waiting, so
that the journey could continue without
delays. If the postillion was in a particularly
good mood, he would play a little tune
for his passengers.

Giddyup!

As in the Wild West, sometimes
the stagecoaches came under attack.
The areas near the border were particularly
dangerous because the robbers could
make a quick getaway.

The Railway — In the nineteenth century the railway was the prime symbol of technology and progress. A road pass like the Gotthard no longer met the requirements of the modern age. And so a railway tunnel was built between Göschenen and Airolo. At **9.3 MILES**, it was the longest tunnel in the world at the time.

It was hot and stifling in the tunnel, dusty and dark. Each worker had his own **LAMP,** but he had to pay for the oil out of his wages.

The debris was carried away by a **MINE TRAIN.** The same train would carry the miners to and from the mountain as they changed shifts.

Water power was used to fill large tanks with **COMPRESSED AIR.** This powered the drills and also provided the men with fresh air to breathe.

It is 5,633 feet from the highest point down to the tunnel.

SAINT BARBARA is the patron saint of miners. Her feast day is December 4.

BARBARA

DYNAMITE, which was invented in 1866, has a far greater explosive force than gunpowder. This made it possible for the tunnel to be built in just ten years, although in fact the original plan was for only eight years.

Digging and blasting were carried out at both ends of the tunnel. The final **BREAKTHROUGH** came at the end of February 1880, and the two passages met in the middle, diverging by just a few inches. Even today, experts are full of admiration for the magnificent work of the surveyors.

The most modern **PNEUMATIC DRILL** of the time was used on the Gotthard. It drilled the holes where the ticks of dynamite were to be placed.

Sometimes the miners could only advance with the use of crowbars, pickaxes, or sheer muscle power.

The New Tunnel —

The new tunnel was a sensation, and the news went all over the world. Before its completion, however, there were countless problems to overcome.

The working conditions and accommodation were truly appalling. Many of the laborers got sick. Almost all the construction workers came from Italy, and they were very poor. Although they desperately needed the money, nobody stayed a moment longer than necessary on this building site.

All this progress did not please everyone. The local coachmen, for instance, were far from enthusiastic, because the tunnel meant their services were no longer required.

At peak times there were up to **3,000 MEN** working on the Gotthard Summit Rail Tunnel.

Why is it called a summit tunnel? Because is right at the top and it climbs very steeply.

Work and sleep took place in **SHIFTS**. It was not uncommon for three men to take turns sleeping in the same plank bed. When one got up, the next lay down while the bed was still warm.

The track could not be too steep, and so in order to gain height it had to go in loops. Since there was so little space, the loops were built into the interior of the mountain.

← GÖSCHENEN / SÜDEN

Wassen

Because of the bends in the tunnel, the little **CHURCH OF WASSEN** became famous. The track passes it no less than three times.

The **STOKER'S** job was to shovel coal and assist the engine driver, making sure that he didn't miss any signals, because the driver had only a limited view through the tiny window.

A BREAK IN GÖSCHENEN:
The passengers would get out and take refreshments in the station's restaurant, known as the buffet. During this time the steam engine was supplied with fresh water.

The New-York Times.

PRICE FOUR CENTS.

VOL. XXXL......NO.9382   NEW-YORK, MONDAY, MAY 22, 1882

OFFICIAL CHANGES IN NEW-YORK   LONGEST TUNNEL IN THE   WORLD

EN / NORDEN →

The Automobile —

The railway swiftly conquered the world, but it was not long before another revolution took place, this time in individual transport. The newcomer was the automobile. As soon as the first cars had made their way across the Gotthard, new rules and regulations were imposed to slow down these modern coaches. They would race through the villages, terrifying man and beast at an unheard-of speed of 19 miles per hour. But it didn't take long for people to get used to this new phenomenon.

When the very first car attempted the route in 1901, there were no traffic jams, but the journey was difficult all the same. The engine was too weak for the **STEEP ROAD**, and so the car kept having to be pushed.

Heave-ho!

Go on, go on! First I'll take a break.

From 1924 onward, cars could be **LOADED ONTO THE TRAIN.**
During the winter months, this was the only way cars could cross the Gotthard, but everything changed again in 1980.

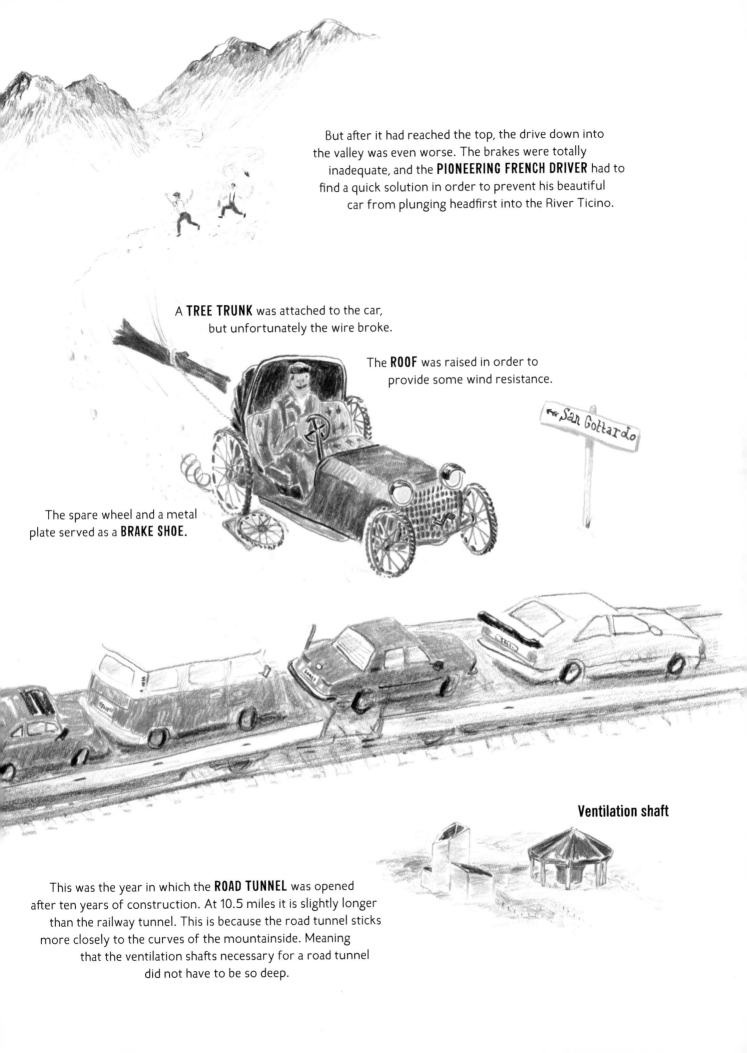

But after it had reached the top, the drive down into the valley was even worse. The brakes were totally inadequate, and the **PIONEERING FRENCH DRIVER** had to find a quick solution in order to prevent his beautiful car from plunging headfirst into the River Ticino.

A **TREE TRUNK** was attached to the car, but unfortunately the wire broke.

The **ROOF** was raised in order to provide some wind resistance.

San Gottardo

The spare wheel and a metal plate served as a **BRAKE SHOE.**

Ventilation shaft

This was the year in which the **ROAD TUNNEL** was opened after ten years of construction. At 10.5 miles it is slightly longer than the railway tunnel. This is because the road tunnel sticks more closely to the curves of the mountainside. Meaning that the ventilation shafts necessary for a road tunnel did not have to be so deep.

The Gotthard Base Tunnel

The Gotthard Base Tunnel — In order to cope with the ever-increasing volume of traffic, the Gotthard needed a new tunnel through which more trains could pass more rapidly. The solution was the Gotthard Base Tunnel. Depending on the type of stone, the work was done with the aid of explosives or with a giant tunnel-boring machine.

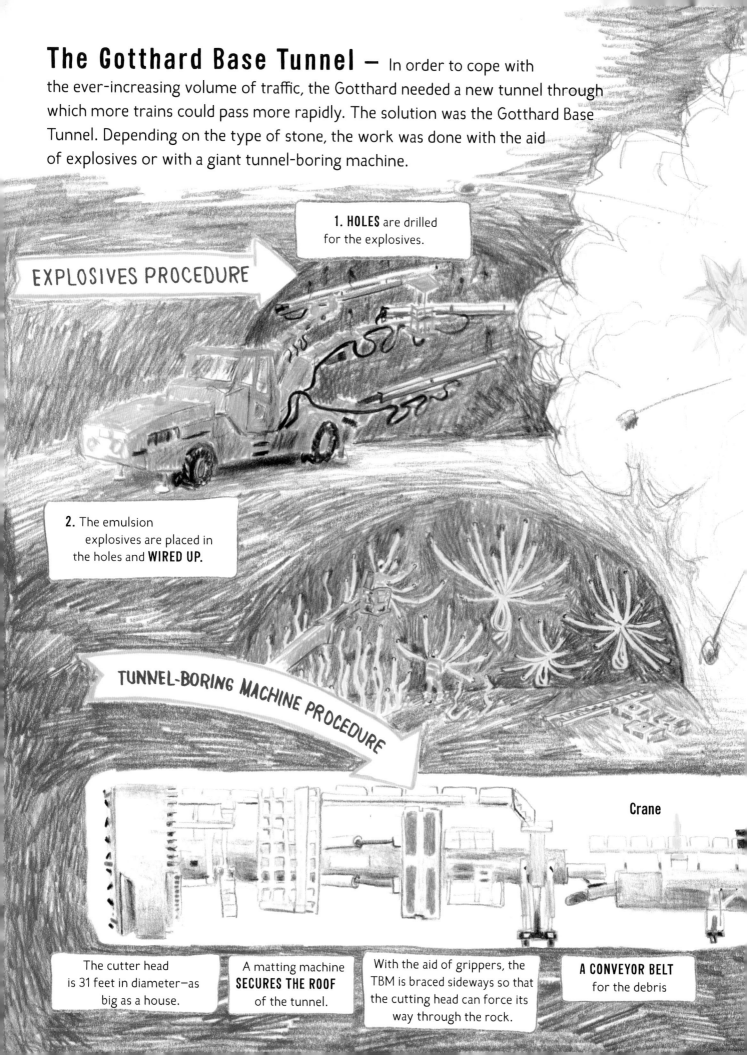

EXPLOSIVES PROCEDURE

1. HOLES are drilled for the explosives.

2. The emulsion explosives are placed in the holes and **WIRED UP.**

TUNNEL-BORING MACHINE PROCEDURE

Crane

The cutter head is 31 feet in diameter—as big as a house.

A matting machine **SECURES THE ROOF** of the tunnel.

With the aid of grippers, the TBM is braced sideways so that the cutting head can force its way through the rock.

A CONVEYOR BELT for the debris

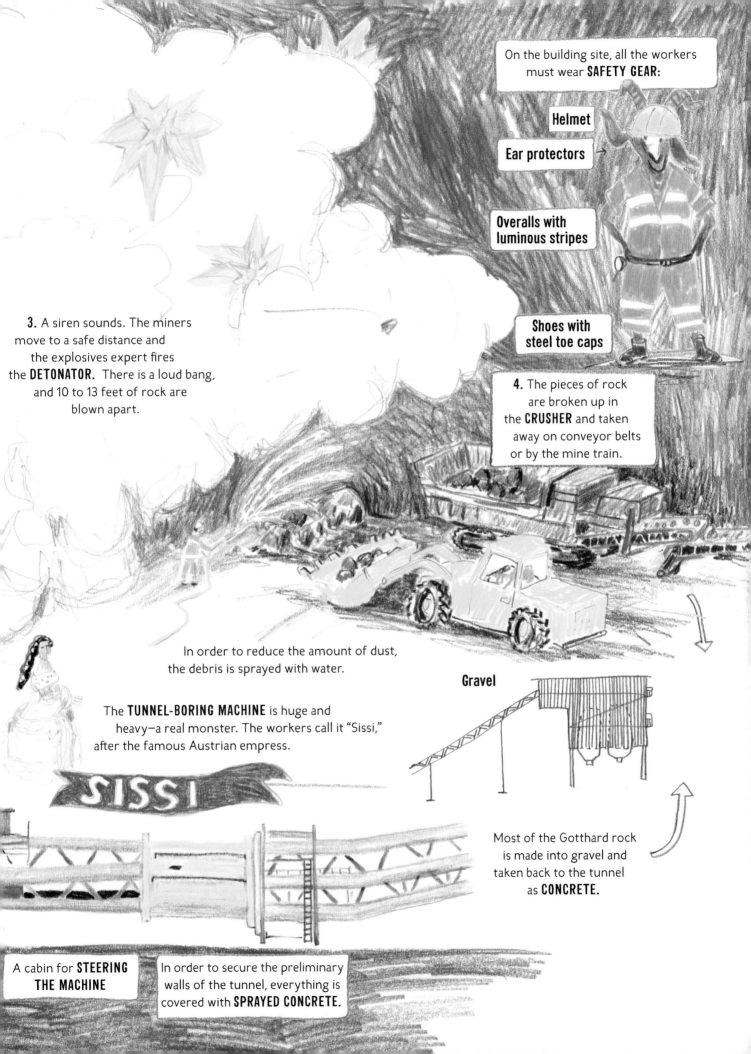

On the building site, all the workers must wear **SAFETY GEAR:**

Helmet

Ear protectors

Overalls with luminous stripes

Shoes with steel toe caps

3. A siren sounds. The miners move to a safe distance and the explosives expert fires the **DETONATOR.** There is a loud bang, and 10 to 13 feet of rock are blown apart.

4. The pieces of rock are broken up in the **CRUSHER** and taken away on conveyor belts or by the mine train.

In order to reduce the amount of dust, the debris is sprayed with water.

The **TUNNEL-BORING MACHINE** is huge and heavy—a real monster. The workers call it "Sissi," after the famous Austrian empress.

Gravel

Most of the Gotthard rock is made into gravel and taken back to the tunnel as **CONCRETE.**

SISSI

A cabin for **STEERING THE MACHINE**

In order to secure the preliminary walls of the tunnel, everything is covered with **SPRAYED CONCRETE.**

Modern Trains —

Mud and dust are a thing of the past. After seventeen years of construction work, 2016 will see the first trains roaring through the new tunnel. At **35 MILES**, the Gotthard Base Tunnel is the longest rail tunnel in the world.

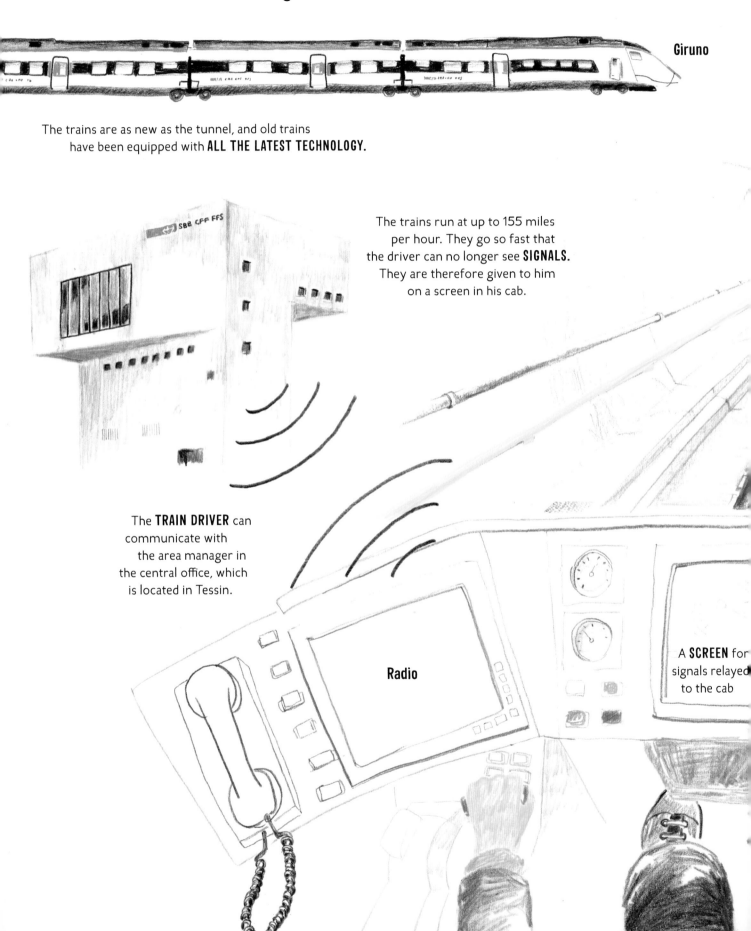

Giruno

The trains are as new as the tunnel, and old trains have been equipped with **ALL THE LATEST TECHNOLOGY.**

The trains run at up to 155 miles per hour. They go so fast that the driver can no longer see **SIGNALS.** They are therefore given to him on a screen in his cab.

The **TRAIN DRIVER** can communicate with the area manager in the central office, which is located in Tessin.

SBB CFF FFS

Radio

A **SCREEN** for signals relayed to the cab

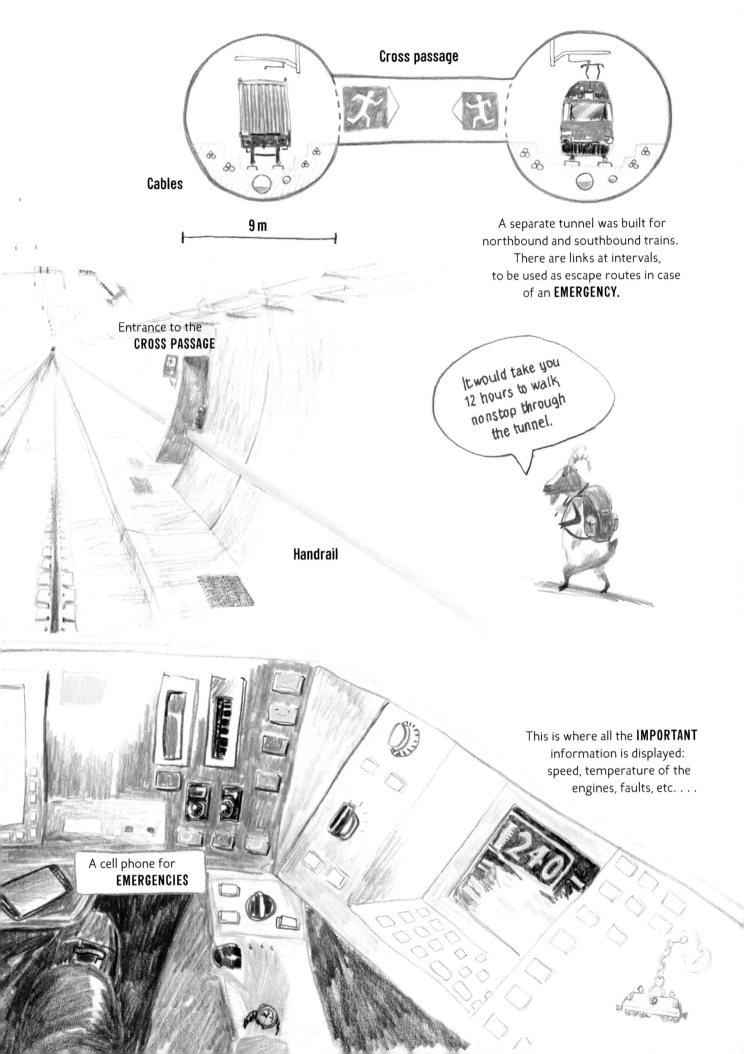

Cross passage

Cables

9 m

A separate tunnel was built for northbound and southbound trains. There are links at intervals, to be used as escape routes in case of an **EMERGENCY.**

Entrance to the
CROSS PASSAGE

Handrail

It would take you 12 hours to walk nonstop through the tunnel.

This is where all the **IMPORTANT** information is displayed: speed, temperature of the engines, faults, etc. . . .

A cell phone for
EMERGENCIES

240

Journey Times —

Back in the Middle Ages, it took 3 days to cross the Gotthard, whereas now the stretch from Lucerne to Chiasso can be done in less than 3 hours. In the course of time, as traffic became denser, means of transport also changed.

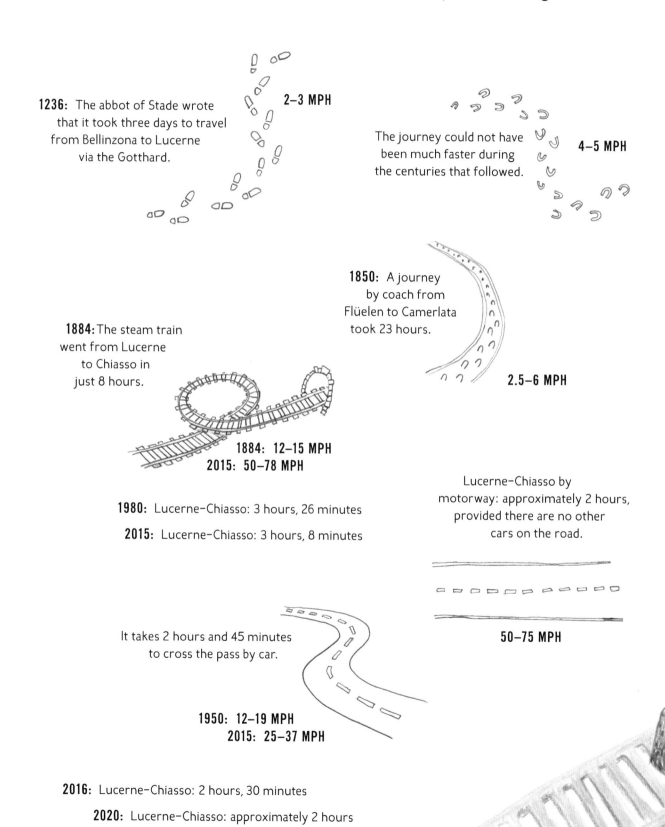

1236: The abbot of Stade wrote that it took three days to travel from Bellinzona to Lucerne via the Gotthard.

2–3 MPH

The journey could not have been much faster during the centuries that followed.

4–5 MPH

1850: A journey by coach from Flüelen to Camerlata took 23 hours.

2.5–6 MPH

1884: The steam train went from Lucerne to Chiasso in just 8 hours.

1884: 12–15 MPH
2015: 50–78 MPH

1980: Lucerne–Chiasso: 3 hours, 26 minutes

2015: Lucerne–Chiasso: 3 hours, 8 minutes

Lucerne–Chiasso by motorway: approximately 2 hours, provided there are no other cars on the road.

50–75 MPH

It takes 2 hours and 45 minutes to cross the pass by car.

1950: 12–19 MPH
2015: 25–37 MPH

2016: Lucerne–Chiasso: 2 hours, 30 minutes

2020: Lucerne–Chiasso: approximately 2 hours

137–155 MPH

The journey is much more pleasant these days.

"We'll be there soon," said Mom, "so let's start packing our things."

"Already?" Emil complained. "But I'm winning!"

"Bad luck!" said Paula with a grin.

"Soon you'll be playing your games on the beach," said Dad.

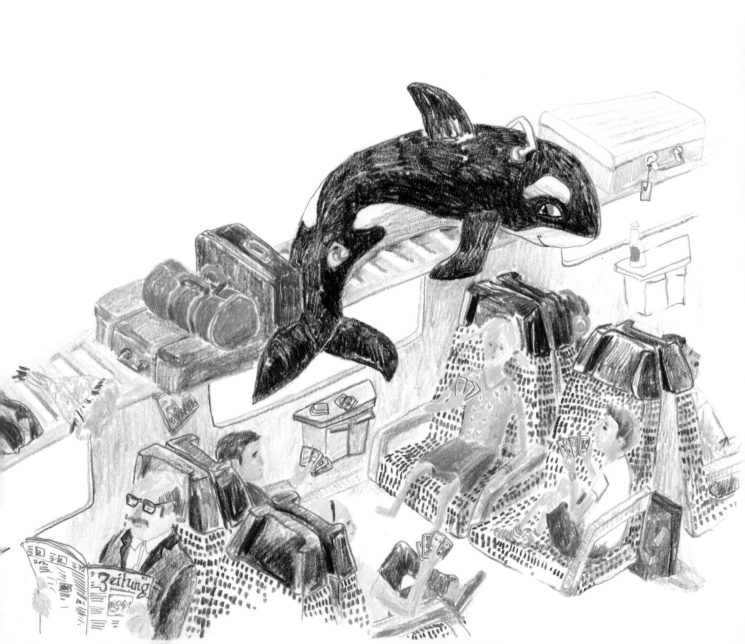